legacy

legacy

Ilene Kowis

Tampa, Florida

Legacy

Published by Gatekeeper Press
7853 Gunn Hwy., Suite 209
Tampa, FL 33626
www.GatekeeperPress.com

Copyright © 2023 by Ilene Kowis
All rights reserved. Neither this book, nor any parts within it may be sold or reproduced in any form or by any electronic or mechanical means, including information storage and retrieval systems, without permission in writing from the author. The only exception is by a reviewer, who may quote short excerpts in a review.

ISBN (paperback): 9781662941832

Jennifer

Jennifer is her name

White wave is what it means

Such a surprise when she came

No Little baby so it seems.

No Little clothes for her would fit

But beautiful she was, we must admit.

He big dark eyes, the great big grin

You know that she will always win

The hearts of all she comes to know

Like the big white waves that flows and grows

Kaitlin

What to say about this special girl?

So much like her mom you can't believe.

Dark hair and big brown eyes

Just makes your hear turn upside down.

She will be a special girl

When she grows up to learn and twirl.

Mom and Dad will be so proud

When they see their girl stand out in a crowd

She grew up so fast

Stand on her feet at last.

Never to forget her wonderful past.

Michael

Oh what a blessing this little boy

He could be a Halloween joy

Born in October, a little pumpkin

He will always be a special bunkin

One day he might say

Why was I born as a pumpkin joy

Your special day, just sit back and take a pumpkin and nestle

He will grow up to be a great man

Probably a farmer, businessman, maybe even the president

Whatever he becomes, he will always be special

A great-great grandson something, no one can change

Our little pumpkin born in October

Our Halloween boy little Michael Roy

Stephanie

One night a star was born

It shines so bright for all to see

It comes out every night

So big and bright for all to see

If you lost your way,

You could always see by the ray of the star that was born on that special day.

Dylan

One day on a street close to home

Around the corner a car alone.

When riding around as they liked

Too close the car and the bike came

No time to call out the boy's name.

We lost our special little boy

So now he's an angel in the sky.

You can see him sitting at Jesus' knee

How special that would really be.

But hard for ones left behind to wait and see

Some day we will all be together

And know how special going home is better.

We miss our special Dylan

But should be glad, no reason to be sad.

He's home in heaven like his fate was made

The day he was born only a few years to stay.

Brayden

Once they are little,

Then they are riddle

Not to know what they will do,

Full of everything new

Go to school, play ball,

Ever so big and tall

Like daddy who never would fall.

Jessica

Just a little dark-eyed lass

Every twist and turn so fast

Seeing her is just a joy

Sitting there with her brand new toy

Inside her heart is bright as gold

Causing her to shine so bold.

Always a precious joy to hold.

Ryland

What a ray of sunshine

He leaves so much behind

No crying or whining

None of any kind

Such a little man

Camping and fishing is his thing

Seeing him makes you want to sing

Harper

What a little princess

She likes to be

But trouble follows her around

So look out, she can be found

Look up or down you'll maybe see

Her on the ceiling or on the floor

Whatever it is, she is the best for ever more

Holly

So bright and cheery,

Soon she will be two.

Flies around like a fairy

Always ready like morning dew.

She's grandma's little Xmas girl

Poppa "Too's" darlin' too.

In our eyes she's like a pearl

Even when she's tired and blue.

She's growing up so very fast,

And every day is one big blast.

Sesame Street is great indeed.

One day we'll take her by the hand

And tell her just how very grand.

She's made our days so much brighter

Each day with her gets so much lighter.

Gracie

Gracie Mae, the quiet one

But sure bright as the sun

Just a lot of fun

From day one until eternity

Will love her constantly for ever and ever

One day she will have her own family

Then she'll know how much we loved her all this time

Isabel

Where do I start; I waited too long.

The words don't come; they are long gone.

Such a beautiful girl with music in her heart.

With grandpa and guitar never a dull moment.

So beautiful the music all day she could play.

Not on earth we can hear her, but angels

Can say she's just as beautiful in heaven as she

Would be down on earth.

Take care of our great Izzy; she's a very special girl.

In our eye down here she will always be our very precious pearl.

Zach

One boy after two girls

Oh my, I wish I had curls.

Maybe the girls would think I was

Just part of the girls that come to do hair.

But when they leave, it isn't hair

In fact, they could not share.

I'm just a boy; they did not care.

Tall and straight, I like to be late

Make the girls really care.

Heather

Once there was a dark-haired girl
Her eyes were just the same
Everyone thought she was a precious jewel
Heather was her name.
She grew so fast; it was a shock
So tall and straight she stood
Then one day to find that she could walk
No baby left to cuddle and coo.
Course one year old is a beautiful time
To enjoy the gifts from a little girl
The smiles, the laughs she gives are divine
No wonder she's our precious jewel.

Gavin

So quiet and still

Your heart will just fill

With the love you can feel

When he comes through the door

You see a great boy

Growing up will be a joy

To see which way he will go

Brody

What can I say

What can I do

Brody is a joy

Special big boy

Faces he makes

The love that he takes

With a heart full to the brim

All vigor and vim

Hazel

This little girl is so smart and bright

There isn't much to say.

A little girl with angel wings

Makes one want to sing.

She has her stories

And she can put you through a test.

She never takes a rest,

Goes and goes; she is the best.

Annie

An angel from the very start
No one more full of graciousness
No one has a bigger heart
Inside she's beautiful, no less
Each way she stands apart
Radiant as a dove
Over and above
Symbol of grace and love
Eternally from above

Aralynn

Dark-haired girl so bright and smart

What will she do; what will she start?

Looking for something to do

Likes animals even those that coo.

Growing so fast no one can see

Always fits to a tee.

In her home with mom and dad

Baby brother won't be long, wait and see.

Robert

One little boy

That's growing so fast

With a cart full of toys

With a heart full of joy

Our truly beloved little boy

Daniel

Never have there been eyes so big

Looking round so not to miss

Whatever there may be to do

No time to waste, just on the go.

A little shy, but such a charm

But strong he will be, to ward off harm

Brave he will be

Like in the early days, you will see.

So his older sisters, they'd better look out

For all they'll get done is to holler and shout.

Blake

Mom and Dad had a long, long wait
But then one night came a boy named Blake
Sparkling blue eyes and shiny blond hair
Such a little bundle of joy to share.
He's going to be a bright young man
I do believe there is a plan
To change the world the best he can
Jut to look in his eyes you can surely see.
That he knows what he wants
And will always fly free.

Asher

There's my boy, what a joy

So happy he could be a toy

A guitar is his fling

And he can even sing

Like grandpa that was his thing.

He's a great little boy now

Be with him a while

Who knows, you may see a smile

We will wait and watch a while.

Jaxon

What can I say

You're a joy today

Such a big boy

You just make my day

Like your brother you like to be

But someday you will see

Maybe like your gramps

Play music all day

A song on your lips

You'll make it play

On your own we will say you got it today.

Sarah

Sarah Ilene, our fair little princess

So tiny and petite, but a heart big as the world

She doesn't sit still, but goes all through the day

Trying new things, sometimes good, sometimes not.

Learning for her is just what she needs

So she can fulfill life's greatest deeds

She is greatly loved but she loves in return

She's our princess, our love, our Sarah Ilene.

Sally

Noble lady, so they say

Maybe later, maybe someday

Now she's our babe so tender and sweet

So pretty and petite

What can you say, what can you do

When you hear her chatter and coo

So special is Sally; so great is her charm

The coldest heart she could surely warm.

Jocelyn

Just our own true sweetheart

Our little red-haired miss

Cute as a button, we love to kiss

Everything about her, she's set apart.

Love is all around her when she's there

Yet so much more to spare

No one like her; you can't compare

Her name means virtuous, supportive, and just.

Love comes from within; she's full of that love

With her it comes natural, with help from above

To see her, to hold her, love is a must.

Olivia

So tall she did go

Beyond and below

Can't keep her so small

One year older comes close to fall.

Whenever it is she has a ball

She likes to be outside

But inside she is a card,

Little Olivia is our doll.

Aliyah

Pretty girl, up so high

With eyes that makes you smile

What a joy it would be to spend a day

With her would be great I would say

Come one, come all, what a joy would be

For sun, stars, moon, what a ray

It would surely pay.

Isaiah

Oh, what a time

Turn on a dime

What a joy you will be when you're grown up to be

Someone so special we have to say

How special, how great

Could this boy your fate

Never will you be late.

Andrew

Andrew came to us unexpected
What a joy to have him here.
Very quiet but, oh, so good.
I'm sure he knows how he stood
In our heart we love him so
Couldn't be better had he started, too,
With all of our kids he's a part of us
So grow up like we hope with no fuss.

Kylee

Kylee is the youngest so far, with big brown eyes
And dark, dark hair.
We've only seen her once, but the time with her was so special
She laughs and plays with such great zest,
Nothing for her but the best.
We can't be near her but hope she knows
She's in our hearts as she grows and grows.
Maybe someday we will all be together
To love and share things we've never had.
Never think of how sad,
When all this time we've been apart,
She's still our Kylee in our hearts.

Madelyn

Such a beautiful girl

Heart like a pearl

So full of vigor and whim

Keeping up with her is a trip.

Piano she likes

She rides her bike

She's just a little tyke.

Bryson

Lives too far away

Seems so hard we can say

Not seen him yet today

Hope he will know me some day

Know that he will be loved

Regardless of miles above.

Gracen and Camden (twins)

Too far away, we do not see

How fast they grow

I know it has to be a win

It can only be a set of twins.

A little girl so special and pure

Grow to be great I am sure

Maybe one who will care

Her brother born the same day.

A big boy sure all will say

His sister will always be a golden ray.

Amanda

Oh my goodness, a special girl
Will be tall with hair that curls?
Pretty quiet but very smart
Will give everyone her heart.
Away from home so miss her a lot
But know we are with her all the way
As she grows and loves to play
Some day she will be a charm.
Until the day someone takes her arm.
'Til then we will love her so
With heart and love, oh so warm.

Grady

A special day for all

When this boy was born

He will grow big and tall, smart and never fall

Always brave and never stall

So handsome he's sure to turn heads

But don't stop doing the best

Will always see him on the top

Nothing will make him stop.

Naomi

How can one explain?

We have a granddaughter who soars like a dove

So full of life in such a short time

She sparkles and shines like a brand new dime.

Growing so fast in a few short months

Even comes up with a few cute stunts

Time goes by so very fast

Little babies, they never last.

One day you will be big and tall

Really, it will be a ball

Don't grow up too very fast

Let grandma and grandpa's baby last.

Thomas

Eighteen years ago this special boy was born

On a bright and sunny morn

He always walked around telling his friends

He had a hole in his heart

Guess it was true. He had heart surgeries

Back surgeries

But he filled that hole with love.

He loved to cuddle when he was small

But liked it when he got tall.

So much love this boy had in his heart

You can't almost be apart

Off to college he went this year

A part of you will always be near.

Stay bright and shiny and oh so clear.

Your dream had always been to make pizzas

Heaven forbid a full grown

Even if you have a hole in your heart

It will always be filled from the start.

Samuel

Bright as a shining star

So handsome and tall, he has a ball

To school he goes in the fall

Getting so straight and tall

Growing so fast, he's a little man

The world to see when he can

Another bright light shining in the sky

For all to see up so high, sigh.

Jonathon

Oh, our little angel with a halo

Sometimes has a devil's grin

But doesn't last long, just turn

On the game.

For the ball is his greatest name

He knows all the players

And the teams

Should be a coach it seems.

Never a player his heart it appears

But won't stop his when it comes

To a game don't fear.

Amy

Amy is our little love

So pure and sweet like a snow white dove.

Beloved is what Amy means

The perfect name so it seems.

The kisses she gives are such a delight

Not many, or often, but with such great might.

So quiet and sweet she is growing to be

Not long she will sit on our knee.

Growing so fast it seems to me

But always our beloved she will be.

Abby

An angel with her wings

Make your heart ring.

Like music to play

So she does say.

Lessons she will take

I'm sure she will make

A beautiful woman someday goodness sake.

Many hearts she will wake

But so beautiful she will be.

We will wait, and we will see.

Katie

What will she be

We wait and see

She loves life to a tee

No one can compare

What she might do

She is so rare

We cannot dare

To think about how she will be

We know she will be fair; you will see.

Ethan

A little boy gone to heaven way too soon

With the angels he sings his tune

So through the stars he flew so high

Only just a big deep sigh.

Like in the sky as sweet as apple pie.

We never got to meet our little boy

But someday we will be with him what a joy

Will tell the angels, thanks for taking care of him

But we'll take over and with such great cheer

We couldn't get to him in time; what a sin

But now at last we can do our part for our little dear.

Emily

What can you say

For someone to play

Always ready and on the go

Keeping up is hard

But so sweet is Emily

She's always a glow

Beau

On Sept. 10, 1995, a little boy was born

Beau Allen was to be his name.

Dark hair and fat little face

So much fun every morn.

He will be the name of the game

As he grows and grows at such a pace.

With two older sisters he's bound to be loved

And Mom and Dad to see him through.

All the good times and the bad

Things so great from above.

He will always be true

To those who love him, no one will be blue.

Kyle

A special young boy
So full of joy
So bashful so like a little boy
A smile, a hug so quiet he is
Never a word or a complaint.
In the kitchen he is a whiz
But a prayer is good
As a young man he stood
Tall and straight he will go.
A smile and a hug
Just gives your heart a tug.

Alia

A little girl grown so big

Where does the time go?

The angels would know

With her they stay.

To follow her all day

To keep her so she won't fall.

She will grow up to be so tall.

Destyn

Little boy that looks like his dad

At times he looks a bit sad

But don't feel bad as he can get mad

A little boy so sweet and so glad

To have Destyn good or bad

No one could ever be sad

To have a boy that looks just like his dad.

Zander

What a little man

Looks just like dad

Likes to play whatever he can

What a handsome lad.

Never a dull moment with him on hand

Our little boy playing in the sand

Would like to go all over the land

To see where he can make a stand

Kennah

Our little girl came to us a bit grown up

So special she was like a little tea cup.

She's growing so fast you don't dare look

Pretty as a picture in a little book.

In school already she goes every day.

Little babe, she cannot stay.

So bright she is at the break of the day

But growing up she's on her way.

Lanie

Her name is special

An angel there to see

With her I'm sure it will be

So sweet and pure and free

One doesn't think beyond today

That a rose will brighten the way

As Lanie Rose can do, we all will say

Spencer

What do we say, what do we do
A girl to be, we thought we knew
But Spencer came to us one day
Like a small reflection of his dad
Everyone was so glad.
Another boy to love so dear
So strong and bright, have no fear
Lean and tall Like Mom and Dad
A star, no doubt, and never sad.
Happy unless it's food he needs
Maybe a star someday he will be.
Whatever his future, he will succeed.

Mitchel

What a special, special boy

Very shy but what a joy

Growing up so very fast

Not sure just what he wants but know it will last.

He's going to be a special young man

We know by the way he plans

His toys he moves like they were real

So to watch him grow is quite the deal.

Video games he does like

But always ready to go for a hike

Comes back for his games he likes

Must be good as he may even scream yikes.

Ashlynn

A beautiful star in the sky,

Like a piece of apple pie.

Sweet and tender, never hear a sigh

Happy to go out in the snow

To rock and roll.

Ready to help her mom so good

Put away all the food

Babysit her sister, no matter the mood

Always happy there she stood.

Ian

Oh, what a treat the day that we meet

So dressed oh so neat

Hair to die for cutest smile

How special is Ian, how special the style

To see him you'd walk a mile.

Sophia

I wonder if Sophia is a sign we need to show us the way

On this special August day

What a beautiful sight to see; a little angel came to stay

With the name of Sophia Rose, you see.

What more could we ask for when we named the dove

But a ray of sunshine that goes deeper than love

No virus, no fighting; no, not any one; just an angel come from above.

Zoee

Such a star in the night air
So tall and straight and fair
What will she be
Can't wait to see
Dancing she is a charm
Always ready to go no harm
Pictures she can draw
Goes on anything, even a saw
There's ornaments and jewelry
So great, you see
Even masks for you and me
Always ready to lend a hand
Take her and make a stand

To the Unborn Babies...

"We should get out of here," one woman said.

"But it feels so safe," another said.

"You have two to three months left, and I only have a month," the first said.

"Say, you two have only got a week," a third said.

"I'm a little scared; I don't know who I'll meet," the first said.

(*One week later...*)

"Well, you guys, this is great! Mom and Pops are super. Great Gramma went to see Great Grampa; Grampa went up a long time ago," she said.

(*Future grandkids, great grandkids, great-great grandkids, etc.*)

"Great Gramma is the one writing about us.

I guess Grampa used to sing and play the guitar.

Sure wish I could have heard him.

I can't wait to get there if it's that good; I'm ready to go.

They all love us and tell us stories about all who couldn't be here.

They say to always say 'I love you' after you talk to someone.

They say that is what makes a family."

"See you on the other side," she said.

www.ingramcontent.com/pod-product-compliance
Lightning Source LLC
LaVergne TN
LVHW051226070526
838200LV00057B/4627